The Dyzgraph^xst

a poem

Canisia Lubrin

McCLELLAND & STEWART

McClelland & Stewart and colophon are registered trademarks of Penguin Random House Canada Limited.

Library and Archives Canada Cataloguing in Publication data is available upon request.

Published simultaneously in the United States of America by McClelland & Stewart,
a division of Penguin Random House Canada Limited, a Penguin Random House Company

ISBN: 978-0-7710-4869-2
ebook ISBN: 978-0-7710-4861-6

Typeset in Centaur by M&S, Toronto
Book and cover design by Leah Springate
Cover image: Sandra Brewster, Blur 9 (3/3), Photo-based gel transfer on archival paper, 30×22 in., 2016/17.
Printed and bound in Canada

McClelland & Stewart,
a division of Penguin Random House Canada Limited,
a Penguin Random House Company
www.penguinrandomhouse.ca

3 4 5 6 7   25 24 23 22 21

Penguin
Random House
McCLELLAND & STEWART

For the impossible citizens of the ill world

CONTENTS

Dramatis Personae

i: First person singular.

I: Second person singular.

I: Third person plural.

JEJUNE: THE VOICE addressed, every page. The chorus, the you, the we/unnavigable self. The character never leaves the stage. The character must always leave the stage. This is an ocean drama.

dys·graph·i·a
/dis'grafēə/
noun
PSYCHIATRY

dysgraphia *by the imprint the link the image displayed through nothing here
| the kinds of given names | the coming away unmarked | the wonder at this
edge if it is I's edge | at this head if it is I's head-full of a disappearing act |
assembled cautiously in I as those children of today | as the mouth turning out
the speed of sound-now | in this 6: 21 am breeze with someone
maybe you still alive with familiar irresistible mystery where I choreographs | the
manoeuvre of to-come and give-way | where the world is full of reasons to push
the back seat down and set a life-force soaring back to its ragged world | to the
ones preoccupied with the ragged that is I | the ragged that implores the ragged
that turns all narcotic and detour | that a thing can name what
it survives in the in and gives hell on the way out*

ACT I

AIN'T I AT THE GATE?

. . . elsewhere called the means by which to burn

X

now   a
common lift

Is it not enough to enter ending, one self in the halving road,
and the fires in us blot the coasts that reject us and we sugar
the desert we screed, frantic for fullness, if fragile, if symbols

if nothingness, at first a doubt escalating our verbings,
if still ourselves, a thing to become, past wavering interests
in peace, given only for spilling, recall that face which is no face

a craved choice, eureka in someone's drawn god, I and the next
could praise now if I were not set ablaze enough, if that morning
i hadn't the thirst to lean into the world with an ear to a mouth

begging for the happened thing, for something disguised, what could
prove this dust is freshly mouthed, not some cyclic newly vaporized
empire settling its faithless wages: I's masses, these bent backs, enough

mwen ni malè, ma ni lè, that never-ending soukou, sé-sa
nou, this is it, our deadland, raw as the last bomb leaves
our storied hand, kité nou la, which mother té manjé yish,

look, we (a) conversation (b) pointing ceaselessly homeward,
whose earth is left without a means to unwant us in place, why
we sing-back anyway, the chaotic corners of mind after wretched

mind, who is left after the dysenteries, after the cities and the ruining
magic we no longer believe, a dusk we no longer need, what is I
but to always have been (t)here, I've asked it, what is I: I in an own place

I is here breeding out of the deadland a definable origin
where everyone is—yet-to-be-named equipment, as if whole
where news of uncut humanities discarded—whole, islands

made of antagonizing food—lift today—Pacific Ocean, tomorrow
Indian Ocean, and then another tomorrow another ocean
surge clearing wave, where nothing is open, where things exist

to be drawn outward by singing, how nakedly the dawn spills
or lifts in the responsibility of doves emerging with their late-
summer songs in early June, I wants none of the peril, unless

to flag a bush-one risking the dark in me, in the voice of I's
mother, in bacterial forces' unbelief, the stoppages of one
maybe two hundred stages of rupture

as I enters the current blank-shots of work, I leaves the Baltic
zone in its cubicle and seabed, unchanged, why de-escalate
the science from its pain, some Westerly continent is paramour

the minute I must resolve to process the rate
at which to belong to whatever, the speed at which to
spring the codes of stoicism from their pure energy

a ruby caught just barely in that one earlobe
I lusts after, I has crossed the hair-like perimeter
giving a fuck, like a press-ganged submarine crew

marching moss-grown intentions in a vote, the obligatory
panacea against Napoleonic time meaning bested nausea
meaning desire into threat of illness or expanded lives

I would like to find lodging the world depends on,
some craft of soil and seashells unafraid of robotic
futures; what is any of this to the characteristic poor

and the woods pull out their hair as I slants something
like a route, I stagnant, uncommitted to the scrutiny
of another passerby adrift in their love-drunk uncertain self

before one woman sucks another woman out of an accounting
into hunger for #prisonstrikes, I is a quick slash on the tongue
drawing the head up to read cities out of their bricks' hard-won

lines, their messaging the blocked repose of regular Sundays,
an excuse you already know, what will hold the lines straight,
form the mason's name in its original unoriginal Portuguese

or was it once Italian, once Irish, Yiddish even, superscript
of all the Native tongues gone limp, what I eats, mamaille la,
I becomes: the Créole mouth

hem ya haos blong mi kaye sà là sé sa mwen
him here house belong me
like I's at the gate not like I's a gate

here: plank the tongue that nails year by year a hope to leave
unmarked by this life, this life mortally wounded with unspeaking
still able to make crystalline rock, grow eyes trained

on the roads that turn three walks into grace, or gale, these wrecks
in the Baltic said to belong to no one, in the usual speed of animals
aware giants, too, get lost, children make a disturbance and call to us: come

enter now: a birth, a studied life, reordering of things yet formed,
not yet speech, I could feel two lungs hassling, a hindrance
to what is cleanly wanted (un)rewound, what else is need,

or needed, telepathy then, the millions jostling for space
among all the dead things kept alive, and it's true
the bush-one's at the gate, observing this neuroned decade

in it, was an orange night full of talk
then again at the gate, the double-delirium
of a morning armed to drain the ocean

of its careful frequencies, limbs turning up
all this fanfare, una gran función: all I wants
is to kiss any forehead still wet with no false

innocence, what I believes will raise mercy
against all this hesitation, all this public applause
and I regrets to think someone will erase our ex-

periences of this world just to push I out the crest
of it and to make something beautiful of it
now yellowed with waking, I quails, but speech

the unhearing that gives I the true world,
the mouth out of shape at the saw-toothed cliffs
of Morne du D'ore is a becoming: the green centre

of where to grow after refusal, the big entering
the small that cleaves what I has
not yet been driven mad for discovering

I pulls off I's toes and leaves them near the sea, I's sea,
back to the sea as before, yet an hour's drift from
Manzanilla, which is no place but a word I loves,

I knows what begins the act of saying things, what is lodged there
a promise of some life, not unlike this coal-grey sky, not unlike
the not-good marching band a street away throwing madness

out with I's lonely discography, I says "please," without toes
but what about these feet now that they are not ceased
in their act of marking things, disappeared things

things given over to the gesture, the method, to the field
awash and undertow, what is love but the hand returning
to claim the dust red, white, black as a coal-swept evening

here a burnt mountainside, seasons setting aside their obscene openings
I who's only ever sensed these three yards before a stiff trunk shirks off
its tattoo of ringed wisdoms or maybe years, yes, all that they are

in the mouth's vain muscle, a family in a struck way budgets the death
of their vagrant cousin to the obsolescing tar, nothing like a sentimental
drudge through the what-ifs, nothing like a morning so unclear as to leave

I before the opening I knows where to find, unlike the cousin
who has been missing for a decade: ever, where I should forget
I's own vagrancy, who were you before I, speaking of beginnings

here—beginning the unbeginning
owning nothing but that wounding
sense of waking to speak as I would

after the floods, then, after women unlike
Eve giving kind to the so-and-so, trying
to tell them it is time to be unnavigable,

after calling them back to what
the tongue cuts speaking the thing of
them rolled into stone

speaking I after all, after all theories
of abandonment priced and displayed,
the word was a moonlit knife

with those arrivants
lifting their hems to dance, toeless
with the footless child they invent

here I wanders into a court in spring
desperate to keep the word for self-
record where the water is broken

with lilies floating like chapeaux and
coming back like women softly singing
the singing spectacle in itself, all of I

passing among them, what can be holy here
if I's troubles are not with god, as they say,
I is prepared for the barbarous trembling, how it could end

here at the edge where the others in the wake
feed themselves agave, the heaven they know
beginning with syrup, their hairs

retreating with the data of nuclear bomb tests
who will make humour in this nervous, tangled play
in the last act, of course, to be unlike anything happy

living as I knows, layer upon layer, no, living is
continuous, what grows within, studying to be let out
to beguile I as alleged or a sewn mouth, or what could be

whole, or life, or lust, or diagnosis, a more flawless
name for I, who wants to keep what you are after,
where I walks the split-tongued edge begging for nil

like the dinosaurs, yes, those who heard the waves
but seeing nothing in the darkness, not yet anyone
swallowed into the twenty-four-hour clock

here you and I both hear this and you find in I
nothing you want, nothing that can be easy
with I as a starting point as you then cast I

to chronicle, to scrub words into timesheets
call I the narrator, but wanting nothing
of the enzyme turning speech

into carcinogen the minute air meets it
in the mouth, a half-headed thing remembering
to hoove the human, a last act of self-preservation:

undying fiction, something begun in pre-curse, formless
as though hungered from mutant offerings, I's people,
to victors with names like Somerset, but what about Jejune

Jejune has known I, they were children once
children holding their heads up at the aquarium
of ill-conceived enterprise, let that be all you need

to know, the dyzgraph^xst must lend the mouth
to the flood of oil beneath the Gulf of Mexico
the waves doing their best to save us from Amerikkka,

the premonition of coins, given plumage, red, jaune, blé ek
owange, the children who know their job: know to never be
done with answering the unanswerable: di nou ki les ki la

to never raise a hand or shield themselves against
some agent of decay, lithographic forms of having
to commit, to commit to the speaking, bluer

than perpetual lines of black tears, you meet I,
now the elder one, wanting a haunting with Jejune
though all of that is too much, too much to ask:

it is difficult to live in the dark, I knows
the dark is difficult as abandoned artefacts
abandoned artefacts like graveyards of ships

in the blueprint of wrecked wars, wrecked wars
known to Jejune as the eleven lost in *Deepwater
Horizon*, oil and gas, ignited for forty-eight hours

in sixty thousand gallons of the dark, permit an escape
to the engineers still alive and brave in this dark
then stop immediately, man, then hit I again

after eighty-four days a facsimile, be sure to offer milk then
ask Jejune whether I will cry if you die, whether something
of the pirates and all the ones they sold live (t)here still

de causa naturelle de causa nostra, lay I, now the younger one,
bare in thoughts, bare in I-complications
Jejune does not want it paid in simple-tongue

but let I go, given the choice now to speak
after five hundred years of dysgraphia
let I approach the witness stand in any chosen language,

let I bend into a touch of the supernatural, let that be all
you need to know, where the heart is bruised with unfeeling,
to delay the organ's devotion to devotion, is not belief, or it is

calling I to walk out of the sea, all of the world hears
the surf supply applause, hears Jejune swimming in,
Jejune outlawed in the notes of fifty generations

far from that door of even more (un)openings,
how to pay for the vocal injury I feels at the end of
the Gulf of Mexico, the won wrecks, seeds still in jars after

a century, how the sea hacks the compass still
I feels how far is left to go, Sudan, Abaco, Aleppo, still
before the self-same notes of dead musicians consider I

more than the pen, and to have never thought of
the notes as autobio, and to have never built
a better world to inhabit or break, speaking Jejune,

I has screwed up, I knows it, and how to pay for it
instead, I hammers the joke's humourless record
with a love, a marrow

and what is marrow if not the loss of the right
to scrub vein as words clean, the work is honourless
preoccupied with definition, the work is always to understand

of course, why else the brain, why else the heart
sending blood upward, why else here and everywhere
everything still erupting and unsayable

Jejune knows it is other people who cry out on the news
who risk loam and life on treacherous waters, a homing
to spread the years on a couch and be caught

in a comforting web of verdict: later Jejune leaves her eyes
with a letter that they be laid down on pillowed-pills, dear suicide,
dear vex, dearsex, two-minded, something better fissure mutely

so when they find the eyes and they say, *look*
someone's eyes are left (t)here, here also
is a whole banana parsimony in two hands

in the mind, release I, as though the birds, sure,
to return across this distance exposed
to the sunlight, even as the bridge will be gone,

even as the mothers and all landmarks for rest
declare the mainland the just-waking fort of beasts,
you are so seen, so clear Jejune, given to I before a court

Jejune understands, the signature will wipe I out, I, as the
tobacco'd air, the tongue-tied heaviness of striking this act
of permanent residence with debris given to the children

who ripen to vitamin loss, somewhere far off from Malawi
from Manzanilla, who else is a mothering anagram, Jejune,
who keeps the cloth rough to investigate its lure of an origin—

pushing these fallen few facts seven dozen yards away
Jejune invites the council, or jurors, others even impossible in
their constitutions, for wine to ease the work through the yea

-rs it would take to pay for sense, between reasons to arrive
why else would living be continuous, check here or any other box,
the judge reminds Jejune to arrive without a reservation

to hold the judge to the work of a body astray, Jejune, now waking
the judge arrives (un)flagging the morning understood
in this drying version of a faith, and to be Jejune, Jejune must speak

without the counterfeit luxury of many zeros that I will be loved
and as long as they both shall live yet with some sedition and
god-knows-what   struck through a self

but love, it is one hour before the morning ties
your tongue to every tercet here, one hour
before the loved world arrives by the wild of our tongue

the talking of atoms ninety degrees from the sun,
return, now, Jejune, in this palette stretching a hand
to whatever symbol is an exit, Jejune, expel these gallstones

forgive I I's stealth and true enough explain these least
remembered things are beyond defence where no one is
born well enough pristine except in dreams, of course,

where language is kept clean, for the girl here still wiry
hiding a meal in the white tree, sure that no one will find it
until Jejune, fourth of the ordinary faults the last hour has misplaced

first of the name

yet to be great in this gathering
the voice must bend toward apology,
the tiredness of growing (c)old,

invade the wages of simple deaths
"sorry," Jejune says, Jejune is sorry
but for whom and what has I arrived

for whom does this dam fill the sky, these
molecules blind-eaten from that distance-as
everything I learns about disappearance rains

lifetimes spent in this catastrophic crowd
so what, if a wormhole, so what if the woman
who wakes with Jejune is reduced, irrigated,

salted, harvested, and thrown again to exclamation
points motored in the desert, with no word for anything
needing built by hand, the mechanism of the spray

planes showering powdered milk into the ville I remembers
the lake clotting and Jejune disappearing into drought long
before starvation, long before the woman whose children live

a whole particle away from theory, whose footnotes lodge the throat,
the hours, and provoke Jejune to marvel at our good fortune
next to mothers with all their wailing annulled, somehow,

the motor towing Jejune this whole while, this thing big enough
for laughter, an exhumed patois, Jejune never asks it why
Jejune only defends I: what do you have and what have you tried to save

Jejune, are you here where the day feigns its beauty outlive
our failed reunion, catching I on your tasselled edge,
that February in Toronto, a piecemeal idea for someone

I believes in, a whole month full of ordinary hand-me-down
Sundays, what good must come, Jejune, wait—don't answer,
rest here in this sentence where nobody knows I, or you already

take this road to the mouth, with I after I holding you to
your better nature as chameleon, merely a shade awake
stick your tongue out to the rain even through this garden,

where no garden grows, no strawberries have left seeds to-do, scrap
this smuggled demesne down to the size of a retraction of our steps,
inside the I is a word and a being, inside the being a peculiar thunder

rusty aftertaste of measuring and measuring the miraculous whose
version of this life we lose to a terrible twist: how much trust
to have in the idea of our voices altogether calling home calling home

ACT II

AIN'T I NICKNAME FOR HOME?

. . . elsewhere called a matter of fact

XX

lift

    the self

trace amounts of melanin settled
in that bathwater making mould
in the kitchen sink, the son slaps a hand

on the surface and every quay closes
before dark, Jejune hopes heirlooms
like these will distract I into losing track

of the stories I has heard about the windowsill
with the father's jars with the golden apples
and the mango chow poured down the gutter

turning homeward on a foot two shoe sizes into adulthood
Jejune returns with fire in the veins, with a voice dug up
from the middle sea, hitting the market crowd as stones

in the spirit of recklessness, in the 401's meandering
and all the shortened lives arrayed as welcome, though
it is not a welcome that Jejune seeks, nor dangles from

bare hands, set to the work of measuring the distance
between I's hips and the descending wail of city women
in the middle of the square I says: *touch anywhere and begin*

or press enter, Jejune, exhume I's tongue from the buried
records as you'd asked when we were ten, except do not lob
it at the floating hand I sent there a decade earlier to wait

because now, Jejune, you must hand the beacon
back to I, cutting red a road through this border
before the hand with its index pointed at the temple

of the complete world realizes it is not always foolish
to rouse a sleepless thing, to offer pills for it to stay
awake, to witness the columns of ash and smoke

taking the tsunami by surprise, just as the gods
who sell their dead to stay awake,
before the concrete slabs close in on promises

for doing better, involuntary hours of driving
towards debate, the self for minutes and hours
forgets about survival and heaves a beauty

from the radio, Aretha Franklin today, another voice
tomorrow, that desert sugared with these wrung
selves, we rush and shape stone, not carried

but accrued, where I layers its new language taking back
the miserly mouth, mouth that sours the pot
in our bigbeautiful bigbeautiful

ain't the monstrous always intimate
and before any protest turns it inward
inmate into a vineyard, ain't there a moan

digging one thousand years into the past
as by this interruption: do you accept
this collect call this collect that call

accept the charges how, I, now the daughter,
is here forgetting the voice of her father
or whomever the father voiced

magnum me facit dominus, dwindling
away some rubbery word for fire
or a glance back to something sincere

Jejune, all of these words inflate our undivided lives anyway

and offered back, fashioned as a window
diminishing I into something like wind
across language, across the cello, across

plastic stretching for miles out of our finger-
tips, Jejune into thesis now so-called
cunning before one I as extended ablution,

toward, maybe the lightning that drew
new corridors across the sky, Jejune,
now that you are here, can you tell I

apart from this country belonging to nothing
this far bled and no further, from the still unheard
reams I must enter, this great hall, a summiteer

already owed o deo dominé, a fading agreement
before a hoard, jurors, powdered and wigged,
titrate   and   promulgated,

meaning well before this wide togetherness
of what is simple, spores for atonement
in the age of sleet a single ounce was enough

to end the father I must defend
what's a duty done
what's a word that will do

, does I bring more than that, Jejune,
say the bulk of broken bones between
these hands that cannot mend them

yet, it can't be that, no line is so straight,
it mustn't be the years, scribbled on already
turning against that child illiquid with touch

into something of a personhood, nothing, worse,
what is some faith in neurons, in the intangible
quarrels of having and letting,

in I's grey mood, to have not sung need, common
soil, to have needed the abacus gauging the art-
eries of a dead heart, careful to take its holes

its chambered script for whole notations
whose words make a return to the call
of man-o'-war doved through a clogful age

can you reach, Jejune, between the small hour
and the gathering, and pluck I out before a
duel to the death: is that not why you came

Jejune, are all of these words asleep this century anyway

so now I counsels at the inroads, how to cart through
what could be too much to confess, raise a hand
if you know what kind of body lives in another

kind of mouth, a whole life with the same friends
in the same house, the same lovers
dance of the same dance, to have eaten the same,

the walking, passing, sobbing, the same
dog-crowded parks, black and pink beaches,
some love for words, the mod script of algebra,

language of oil, a madhouse, reel, watch with deafness
the gabled roof, fences, cars, the many-rooted book
—so that is enough, as all exception must be

refuse that entry into this collection,
if all of this sophistry is meaningless
speech branching out of shipwreck

some altered sense, Jejune and I and i find
the highest point in the city, we rub our eyes
with Juniper and thought-of states

merely recognizable by their vulnerable curves
into nothing, or nothing of what was said
before survives, past a tug, not persuasive, but a tug

on exhausted neural membranes
crossing streets, cutting a new ideogram
for volcanic jackdaws, all of the journey now

the fate of everything dubbed   unclean
and we vote to enjoy the view that we know is
indifferent to our love

Jejune, all of these words are our dark twin anyway

so what is the point of the judge in that case
where the father confesses what is better than to conspire
with who would free I or Jejune or any number of us now

a blend of tempers, some crest of white hair, no, ain't
is too much thinking to ask, whatever I is *is*,
do not think I not enough, or too much

of an invention like the wheel like the clock
too much of an invention like the wheel
like the clock that bears repeating

these cracked elbows, the only sign of time passing
at the junction where Jejune leans into
I, with hands ready to feed the open-mouthed self

what of anything is like charcoal, lit like what fails
the sketcher's hand, not a tint impaired, in the sun-
bright past, like fucks is only more robust than memory

who can ask for this long companionship
the least gravitational offence in any hemisphere
how much longer will I fill this long ampulla

of somebody's wor(l)d, who is worth that much,
who is ever this true, please, you do not
ask for too much that the mechanics

should not conceal the message, or concede
the foreclosure of lost generations to a clause
the message is concealment, what more can be taken, spared

now even with a percussed tongue
I can put the world back together
with the twisted timbres of a ship

from some unknown century,
okay, maybe give I some spices
give I the whole shape of a meta-

morphosis to wear, give I
the Labrador Sea and
the nine hundred feet

between the black skein and
the blow it dislodges, give I
the sharp and weary self

give I your infant's breath
a cleanly locatable thing
a clearly thinkable thing

none of it is pitiable that I speaks
the too many clever variables, the
heart-worn brain-shorn light that

clings newly to those friends choosing
to go alone, all of them grasping for sun,
now boarding the dark boat or the freeway

Jejune, all of these words lift a hand to canopy the nonworld anyway

as though time owes us something, but I knows,
time is still a small person
worn-out of dimensions

time's tenses are trades for smugglers, who knows,
why should anybody love the small and wearing
bandanas, now the judge, I must leave but I knows

I is never leaving, I walks briskly past the man,
white-haired on the wheelchair at that door, wearing
gaps for teeth, his cheeks swallowing the pre-dawn dark

do not mention the mother in the morning,
only the wind as the man's only greeting
night through the day since June 1965

does I go past him, I does, wet and exposed
I wonders: is the man a father,
Jejune, what sense is there in such interrogations

or in time, in what tense the man is keeping time
for I, again,
against this palmless clasp and a better judgment,

I returns, I rests one tired hand on the man's
bare head and I does not mention the salamander
or the parasite from 1992, Jejune, then the doctor

expunged, I cannot know the depth of its poison
going this way let the man mistake I for home,
the confessed compromise of the father, then

the killing plot, the Mary Jane worth jail time,
now given a stately stamp and other things not
enough, like love and folly and now I is otherwise again

Jejune, all of these words are a waterlogged birthday anyway

except to be wrong again in this
(un)thinkable season unbearable
cause entreated by swales of violinists

the thinkable novels I speaks in a look
to jolt him alive, to jolt us, me, ah, there,
finally, standing among the seated, *i arrive*

i wake remembering nothing
but the locomotion of lips, maybe mine
maybe the page and some faulty language

do not excuse me, i am not what i say
i have become the clearing wave
open, i exist, yes, but where am I

as much as I can enter
these terms of feeling
i know, here I am fiction

I won't come back now
from imagining into I
there are worst fates,

I understand, here I am
the burned drop
of that telephone beep

ACT III

AIN'T I ÉPISTÉMÈ?

. . . elsewhere called the transaction of dream and return

graphisme
nom masculine

graphisme *sont la manière de former les lettres, d'écrire, propre à une personne une écriture d'un graphisme arrondi la manière de dessiner, d'écrire, considérée sur le plan esthétique le graphisme de Odutola ou Basquiat j'suis pas parfaite or who else is here, here: a second chance the present study is an attempt to place within please bring some patience no philosopher lives here j'suis une edition limitée*

graph·ics
/'grafiks/
noun

graphics *or illustration merely use diagrams in calculation and design unless such a calculation eschews all future responsibility to an ordinary means to an end and there provide all the necessary labourers who scour the field for any thought of redress a figure or any list of reasons to adhere to an arbitration for assassins to exclude one from the known world and from our-self the end itself no further*

X^xX

utterly, utterly

DREAM #1

                              mooring the first stretch of open field
                              to a cycled selfhood, is to know that self
                              without bowing without a gesture
                                          to the ganger's
                                  tent   pitched
                              leaning the luxurious palm

RETURN #2

What am I to make

Of two or three small sons

Of anger with its talent for mixtures

Of thank yous that slide on the present-like a sl/hope

Of the sweetly ordinary: take this small son, his red wafer

Thin chalk drawing of the other son, them making things making

White hymn of all the hymns to all the sons, and what by this green world

Up as early and as well as anyone, up until Uphood, as well the bee, the kawé

In the drizzle and in the tune of the dragonflies and in the tune of the two or

Three small sons lit up with the same charge of what the world heaves in

The night desks and the advances of the lost who leap into age, father

Into a mother and an honest word for keeping the talents

Whether or not to combine whether or not to bring

Anger with the small mass of a clean life—small

Son and so on, present-like of what

What am I to make

DREAM #3

says you, too

live borrowed

on minor eases

you bow before

the nulling wall

lower every hurt

so geometric, every

crude word a hard

line in the dirt, I

will talk less

the perseverance,

you'd like what else is that wounded sense

of kneeling, or else waking up diffused

funny as the need to be more explicit

funny as the scathing and still

to decide to play

a joy

in the unlocked note already enough This sweetness is atomic Is candlelight or
conflagration Say you are wise to be alert Say please look out for strange
metaphors seeking lodging in your temple Say they, god-like and impure

RETURN #4

lie flat on the long road bring the pumice for my hard arrival in air after
yielding all the troubled things that breach the waters now as before; as they
who delivered the rainstorm, saying, first realize reason cannot captivate;
what hurdles to take such extreme measures for Only The Things Need
Known; here—take this volta, it is to be kept pristine; say I am where
someone who isn't me sculpts me a legend; grind out a life struck down

by the sudden weight of what the flesh carries to the first checkpoint
upon waking; say you know already how this ends

DREAM #5

If I could just leave the old things to their trembling

If I could leave you to your monuments, too. No innocence

I've known the sharp world and it is imagined and gerund

big enough for all of us, imagined a tattoo up close

on Trappist-1, and I am more than one way to see

the word-world, sizing up the moment by worth of a return

How rude of me to force you on the thing that springs blood

RETURN #6

What about merely the roads, then, or the epiphanic

hour after them, the newest version of myselves

fit to name you a thing, and though I think about you, I'm shaken

I set us a meaning while you weren't looking, I study the language

that would call us home, the same one to calm the baby

here, let me arise singing if that would soothe you

that all I am is evidenced, or else for who, like me,

to stand-in red sap dripping into nib—the match

DREAM #7

an amateur is in the streets.
to the amateur we are lost
and startled. to the amateur
all the people in the streets
are dancing, are only alive
when not dragged. the sweat
of the amateur in the streets
with her clipboard, with her
hips tight against a banner
with the words in bold red
"nothing is better than peace"

RETURN #8

still warm in this waterhole war
-ning crowds away from narrow
& tight genes & no problem, man
this place where worn trousers go
suddenly red w/ dirt, mud manganese
speedboats now cutting thru spastic
fog, pushing from a riverbank's newly
burning sideburn in Kikuyu, still
suddenly Côte, suddenly Yemen &
suddenly behind me a leaping year
abruptly the mäize levelling La Kaye
Gabon, Burundi, Bujudara, Congo
Here, hold this & my problem: & dream

DREAM #9

mi here haus blong a first: I've
entered the motherland & I feel
orphaned / while it is dark I'm on
standby
I forage for breath / meaning new
D is the same old African D / I picture
myself now leaving again, corroded & in-
flight, rusted late with sparks brushing
from my tongue / this cominghome wilder
in Kwéyol / left in a roundabout / the Mombasa
of whose dreams and with Kiswahili pre
-cautioning a clear Créole lifting the tongue
from whitewashed mud-houses
what have I learned of inner lingua
from women (un)eager to peddle
this / all this back for one American
dolla forgetting this same augury:
I have a problem with dream

RETURN #10

fear is an infection in a refugee camp
the Indian poet brings & greetings
from her students, at least the ones
she remembers stumbling out the rear
of her mind as I remember a fence
I was sure I'd never seen fondly weaving
dreams in God's Own Country, a vital
goodness in that world she believes & in
spite of all the hard things I won't bother
listing now, know a campaign ain't worth
shit unless shit stirs the mo' betta, pli mèyè
but what for & for whose sake do I feel
only anger, sweet jolts, disappointment
gone from me and hope ran cold — say
nothing of art, nothing of the variable logs
again, here: I have this problem with dream

they couldn't have gone anywhere if they
wanted, if I wanted, I could collate someone
out of an onion, cutting their tiers from settler
banter speaking involuntarily the names of
poems, memes, some dramatic dogma from
somewhere they hope we'll soon recognize,
slowly, at their back a sapling gives in to gr
-avity though maybe she's right, the world is
this grace, or victory that ought not to unburd
-en me, because all we have done is little good
& that toppling sapling I can't quite stop
imagining: its slash of land, a seed
crossing water below, a burial
for how long: this problem I have with dream

RETURN #12

I could sit in a boat and be cold, fwèt sé
manyè bête yet in this tent, I let you sicken
me with song, I mean you, poet from Cyprus,
to insist in these last days, you keep your fire,
a mod guitar, the impossible early languages
we unearth, how they took our voices and
left us, still encamped, maybe our hope is
in the poet from Finland receding this
caiman in its ripped 2018 & what else to do?
still to be reminded of this unsleeping word
in this unsleeping country north of the Tro-
pic of Cancer; or what god's birthplace, &
of course, this, such a place would be a transit
town gathering us up the embers of failed
revolutions & so what is happening now, poet,
do you make a fine noise of our unquiet in Hebrew
make them all listen & re-think: do the dogs
mind lies? In Española? Do they mind the Black mouth
weeping? Speaking, then? We believe they bark
in Swahili, so no credit here: I have this problem-dream

DREAM #13

like a stack of worn shirts piled before us
sigh in Polish, or the fights that await us
fifteen houses hence in Arabic, how un-
changed the work of anything into shape
a shard, sharp with hope, a look can draw
the missing piece into masterpiece, whole,
Cree it not? Draw these Earths we refuse,
prepare for them a whole existence hostile
to the shopping cart, yet unrealized future,
the spider means to understand this war, &
do i know? What was then has come again,
do I know of the thing that could be wrong
again, the thing that slows and slows again
that hits and hits again, sick-ness & my pro-
blem with dream

RETURN #14

how many ways can you disappear
a people, dignity by dignity, slant
word by slant word, who turn grave,
grave by grave by the curve and measure
of graves after typhoons, cyclones,
the mounting electrowastelands by the fresh-
water, and wrath of tumours as bright
brush on the forehead or covering over knees,
the work of minutes grating against
millions in flooded cities
what garments I wrap this zealous hand in
steering east all through the night, come
the morning I will not be long enough &
patient enough to level the quick word, a
-way out how many ways can you empty
a people, hope by hope, I do not venerate
men. at. all. I have a problem with dream

DREAM #15

draw me the waking up, the grey hardness
of the mind pressed into the early hours
of another house another law, and fog
a brown century before something like sun
-light, what kind of person dreams while
the world petrifies, its pieces sharp & sh
-amed for red dirt and hard mornings
simple: things are hard, you harden up &
a softness that lets you give one thing
lets you walk off feeling some small need
to be not much for symbols anymore
careful to have a problem with dream

RETURN #16

let no Westerners back into this camp
lucid with insurrection
limp still in their childhood, refuge is a guilt
is a helmet still a helmet is a library overfull
with dense descriptions of coming and going
if to agree that this sword of battered words
is sharper paired with helmet paired with boot
helmet only half-full of a shared language logging
the tides half-emptied of reefs and again the pilfered
logs the madness of royal seals, patriotic unthinking
records lead-born & hand-worn
if but to stay & assemble, to which year to return
having been emptied of the need to
dream who will stay here long enough
to exit with me outta them long days
for as long as it go take, I am asking now
& in spite of my problem with dream

DREAM #17

let them say I have seen the long days
I have seen them rising from the huts
as smoke, I have seen them, as forests
turned brown & flat for remembering
themselves, wishing that we had not
factored into their algorithms, & now
I have seen the long days arrive with
Things I do not know, nothing too much
If I'm lonely, nothing too little if I'm
Able to drain the desert & leave the ocean
Empty long enough for a new beginning,
Why have the long days arrived far from
The valley of the kings, still with the mach-
inery bearing the insignia of ruling govern-
ments, what monotonous pride if they say
I drank milk they bought with a fraction
of our natural selection, be-
lieve them such reckless regard for a few
hours over the long reach of us into some
hot place, a future perhaps? I have seen
us with their machinery & watched them
arrive knowing our desires and leaving
with our deaths, and now you have, too
where is your problem with dream

RETURN #18

for as long as we've had dreams
      we've had rivers, for as long as we've
          had fears we've been rivers, we've
               been legions held ransom for our thirst
                    we wake up ready to stay awake to the rush-
                     wild innermost that time can offer us,
                        to the week-old boats that have come
                     to pick us up with rumours[word] of our innocence
                 in sadstrong songs that pile up before the rain,
              the good pungency of wind through the corn &
           once-full creeks, grabbed guns, the vroom-vroom
      of a crushed mood, coming back, as you & and only you
    please you without helmet, full of song, full of wine & just as
you with sword heavy with the ordination of mud worn out of dream to take
up my request:

[word] To lower the blood pressure, keep alive a word

                    for this problem & this dream

DREAM #19

by any right schema in the blood, witness
dream-covered, the earlier you taken out
shaken free over the railroads or again, now
consider the exacting dust blowing
drones down that old road where maps de
-molish every funding model splitting bone
and flesh? let us not talk of the flesh, or sound,
nothing heavy, just the metal doors of sadness
banging, if none of this is beautiful all of us have
yet the used-up horizontal need to consider
to live and again to have a problem with dream

would you find me guilty of dream
with my trousers suddenly dirty,
with knowledge of the exact thickness of the exterior wall of my kitchen,
the Arctic's flooded reservoirs, the seedlings, the bankrolls,
the rusty stalks of corn, all the labouring & the essential leaves
the seasonal floods, the mineraled mud
what you call civilization
still whole without language
would you talk if I talk
of the water, the ships, the whip,
estates, the guns, the guns, the bullets
someplace five thousand years enough
to be undisturbed
someone
someone once told me the story-of   this dream

or just part of the riff, the hi-hat,
the poets in their languages, the
afro-beats, the toiling where the
money is, the power is, why we
still wonder where to leave our
voices for safekeeping where to
find some-one too many today
still named for old hauntings, coll
-ateral still named for whole towns
turned away from reprieve in the
scorching heat of a moneyed world,
dream enough to never blow away
like physics like vining potatoes, an
-other morning to walk out of
bruised but still alive what, then,
is my problem with dream

RETURN #22

how all of these motives
wear my dark dress and
come along wherever I sleep,
curiously unworthy of physical
address, speaking of gold,
anyway, as tasted sun
I won't bundle up my fears
and make of them some
planet's moon for you to grate
that coming century against,
what was human once
must be human again
against your checklists'
counterbalance, driven again
the burn or the coins never
mind my problem with dream

DREAM #23

                                        be wrong long enough

                                        and a growth of arms

                                        in the unmade world

                              go: make it past

                              that scolding threshold

                              with a morning solid

                    as it is a solid two hours a-way

                    anyway, if the sharks, if mud-brick

                    winters, if dolphins, if the fly-

ing fish keep for us the way, let's say

never (forget) the rung atoms, the water,

the weep, the dream, I have a problem

RETURN #24

up early I try not to give
away my hold on air, human'd
in me. I try like an impaled
Venus to not look down.
so if I fall in call it my fill.
call it after-life. see something
permanent. or call it dispossession.
or that I've given up sitting. or
knowing nothing about a way-
through. say out-come if I don't
come out. say my whole life is in
standing in the breeze. is in
this dare to fix some dream—

DREAM #25

as sweeping has the kinship of water

hissing landward, that base-cycle

drawing excess out again

how water moves, or appears to

always come for us holding us

to the problems the promises buoy

& the rains the train slashes past in view

out the window and the water

moving, stilling you to the thing

beyond you, the long drag

of us, a future plump with dream

RETURN #26

the discordant train is a capon

moving fast & could be

a way to die or

could be the way of water

moving into land, for us

all the young who lie annexing

and awake & dreaming, who know

what trouble is this century

while here is a place

& we can admit to love it

sight, while here is a sky
& can we admit to its daywork & its
return

DREAM #27

I can feel   an offer

a voice and the nightwork

merely inviting sightseeing, or   I can

again be the daywork opening dull

if the new forts don't care the sky is dark

what we make of a more basic abundant black

is not the same as marking the intruding   light

or feeling bad, don't name it leftover-sky, interloper

or call it foreign shelter, porous as I am elsewhere   a dream

RETURN #28

I understand what happened

        not particularly well
        Uronarti,
        why do this:: why send
        poisonous butterflies
        fluttering to the feeding
        ground of hawks after
        a night too heavy with _____

DREAM #29

        & these hours where finally

                we demand

the fucked-with be unfucked-with

RETURN #30

father,

make me again^{word}
a disappearance
ask me again
will I cry if you die

---

^{word} first, leave out the fantasy of the discontinuous

some years are newly cysting
some means to see farlong where
I bring the merciless the mercied
the ones the poet says are certain
not the enemy, I bring a small mud
the empty champagne glass
I bring the unannounced
the air craft and target, what
news I bring brings the knowing,
the really happened the not-yet
known, the new again, the version
in the version that was lost,
the version with some years
of growth, the non-pill, the no-mo
and though all of this is uncertain
the mo' betta, the lost, sugar, the lost

the brutal cool of hours south
of the border: here go my failing
nondescript pronouncements
the eye and ear and mouth
here: with the art that lost
life, here a muscle, here a way
to lean gently, moveable sense
what this is I have barely been,
abridged, I have merely paused
on a return, a way or what, listen
you call me an ambulance or leave
me nondescript, leave a sidewalk
or like I said before, just a voice
making music again, brutal, cool

DREAM #33

I'll go back again, is that a return

And when they ask where I've been

I'll have gathered enough miles

In the muscle of my tongue

To give no answer quite so satisfying as *life, you know*

But to say I've comeback

From knotting myself permissive

From leaking enough around my hard edges

From the *give this back, I do now wish to strike at it again*

This *life, you know* all of its lamped days

To have it all come back sweetly

As thankless time in mileage

Making every revolution a raze

Of Dennery Heights

What could you call that?

Back to where. Perhaps I've strayed too far from the epicentre.
Back to where. Perhaps I've overlooked the constant trough.

DREAM #35

[blank] or what the fuck was I thinking?

If given the barracks   dive in

If given the hand   dig

If given the back   make do | bend

If given the afternoon   keep watch

If given the sun   spare no country

If given the tool   skim I loose

If given the giving   sing wind

If given the voice   say so

If given mercy   make do

If given us   give us

DREAM #37

Because now the question
Surprises

Because the question now
Surprises

What now is made up of one

What now is made up of two

What now is a killing of one

What now is a killing of two

DREAM #39

Say to the killing vote

the crashes that begin

every plain call for calm

let me not impose, let me know the avatar

when the offering of

so abundant a palm

a tent or gesture

is ever without

a name: a mother singing us Up, cycling us green and growing, sisters and I
and I the windrush
and the like

across that river, a walk might reveal

the strict anonymous bend

or cracks that open like neglected vats

a lane marked with *such it*s *as of*s

nevertheless I led to nowhere and here

DREAM #41

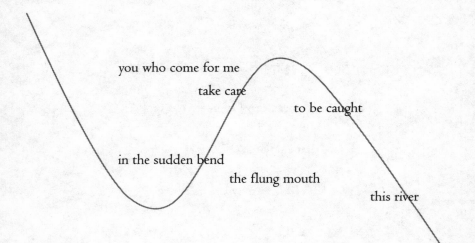

you who come for me
take care
to be caught
in the sudden bend
the flung mouth
this river

ACT IV
AIN'T I THE ODE?

. . . elsewhere called to be

X^{XX}X

new . . .

Jejune is the thought-of
self of the blueprint too
aware of its design

these spore on my mind
on the body of this work
where i see myself pass from

now the fortune
of his survivancy
i stand at an entrance

mouth to protracted mouth
to pass as a father
come back from ever

germ of every note
growth of words—irreducible
as the morning

i have not been written
not merely, but reclaimed
as a clear dress, the same

as any I might share to rise
into seam, steam and seas
hissing themselves sick

there is no cure for this
stretch of my hand back
to the fostered love ringing

in me as a call in me, voices
I ~~virgin~~ against as always
salute the labial ink

some mangled light the colour
of a peace, a sanctimony, a worry
and, yes, some altars that saw me

children that edge out
these lines, each line a regicide
window of circular growths and I
a virgin remembers

unstrapping my spore-layered feet
from my sandals, the saved map
of one, maybe ten or three roads

a freedom to be a thinning
in gradations decrypting I,
whether criminal or defendant

overpass of metatarsals
Jejune:
say smoke clouds my tongue

Jejune, unanswerable, bulged-in
the covert lang that I
should begin and begin again

And all of these words leave the whole ode to me anyway

ACT V
AIN'T I TOO LATE?

. . . elsewhere called exhumations across town

XX^XXX

now log these bones

I remember being is a thing like light^{word},

---

^{word} it arrives and——I breed out / the deadlands, a definable dose of what, good sense, a contemplative note of cachaça to risk us anyway, without cleverness / the stoppages, the nausea, the parchment into hills before

morning and please, no metaphors churning after being / no hurling or finally entering, okay, maybe sopranos' vibratos stuck on E, foliate which belongs to legions, I like everyone / I clear the wave / crease the [_____]

where everything opens and beauty exists as assassin in the bone cured if drawn outward / if it is too nakedly late to address the crow I will insist the dawn into a spilling or a lift / & the irresponsibility of doves emerging with their late-summer /songs in early June,^{word}

^{word} as you, too, sing
the woods, pull out their hair / as though they, too, are aware,
and lust-sharp for life, as though demanding I into the gaze of another /

passerby adrift in their love-drunk uncertain self / before
one new woman who smells like she's ghazal'd a hasty lunch
greets the one who must name her arrival, trip-first; she hands

to the bewildered crowd, I: a quick slash on the tongue, nothingmore /
and all of this I make from a glimpse of my mother in the mirror,
seeing because it was necessary to see, / everything orphaned

returned to famil(iarit)y^{word}

---

^{word} so what has been has been,
and what is a spilling or a lift

if not the cavity where a life
begins, / do not excuse me /
I am not who I say / I have become

I see a black vulture, a fowl
so let me tell you, really tell you, what I see:^{word}

---

^{word} first, the fowl, and I won't claim it

the fowl, not the seeing that I
with the watching can wreck
a summary of, a footnote of,

the bird's bald head spent, all
of its days in the skeletons
of skyscrapers caressing as it must

a question^{word}, blue-suited pigs:

---

^{word} once you are done misremembering
the distended lives as before, and once
I am done watching the fowl, do we:

(a) leave (un)changed, also a vulture,
like a bald thesis in the early morning
before a god is wrung out to dry, or

(b) make out with pointless suppositions, like leaflets?
I want a becoming, the chances of a Monday night
opening into a Tuesday's bright off-loading, you keep your comfort—

like this man at my door with his evidence^{word}

---

^{word} of that world, the known one soon to end;
remember that mothers have eaten their children,
he says, *and so was born the weeping wall;*

I must be lame—is it too soon to offer any
of us forgiveness, what gut-spilling conditions
on the thin edge of even thinner seas

I want that basilisk defiant of sinking
that sleepless teaching into antidote,
a spillage of stitches overreaching for ease,

there's a naked symmetry I am^{word} after

---

^{word} in line on a cloud-cloaked street corner
a beneficiary I recognize throwing vanity

at gangsters with the only correct clock
their hand-shake that means a meal
forget the dust-bound mothers

finally lifting, lifting their hems
with the trembling wisdom of the dog
weary of the scripture of its teeth,

I am that bewildering ceremony^{word}

---

^{word} to be grateful for scraps
how indiscriminate to show up after three decades, child,
springing from these lines, each line a drifting noon hour

do I remember their founding, Candomblé throwing back a song
or two without dealing lesser scales, let them land let them make
no mention of towns full of them dark things, children still camped

in the woods, nursing their broken ribs, from which fall the white
protective cloth for trespass'n the coal mines, yesterday Garzweiler, 2day Appalachian,
the Kanawha River still smokes with the ailing Elk Valley:

how a tongue turns many shades before receiving^{word}

^{word} us
how all a we must fi dead, please, animus: try on
Jejune, I have given loyalty this anatomy of signs

I never learned to walk out of what's mundane,
mere tumbleweed, mind forcing limb
and patois into bridge, some playsome peace

I want no unsuitable offering, no self lurking there –
in stigmata, no, there is no more stigmata
no more malice of that kind,

Jejune, these words are powdered bones along a zebra crossing, anyway paring all-a i-self down to barcode^{word}

---

^{word} that venerated language
of the colony I never got out

of moss and the learned bark
of shapeless pine I am easy to believe—
I've gone from this shelter, left it to the snowy owl

left its skittering snow to translate
the conversion of the burrowing hawk,
remember who chose the black vulture as kin

And I^{word} now the old woman, is

---

^{word} blind with diametric ambition
I am her script: the saccadic vice

of the woodpecker, the glint-wilted
defiance of salmon, or upstream,
the false kingdoms of all required things

I let her trace my face into palm, into terrain
so at least you will know where I have been
though I am no longer prostrate before a fool

some tropical crayfish in her drowned Earth
whose mother knew a woman once drunk
on the words of vanished fishermen, in the biblic'l

sense if I could speak, I'd sing you her name, Jejune,
I'd oil up a body-builder expert at trombone, let you hear
the expreshun she was so quick to utter & let a pulse rip

I hear hurtling, venereal, the click^{word} of a door,

―――――――――――

^{word} or is it just rust I hear in you—Jejune, say nothing
of my birth, fed up at the aigrette on the rivered banks—

which one of us is sure we know nothing and though
restless at this writing toward: whose second glimpse
cuts the moulded saxophone brassing the new

crowd, to make a new phrase for the saxophonist's
buzzing lips, to rip me a cave with horns, I do not talk
its beats so that you will find me again, just that I can be

as I once was: parting a new country as the hard-falling rain

someone's eyes^{word} you left here

------

word with the wing of a monarch butterfly
protruding from a tear duct, radioactive

and fallen on the ridge of a cheekbone,
or a cathedral blocking traffic,
and now the whole banana

economy my hand scrubs means
never to name this derangement
of spent hours, the many revolutions

I have lost, I could not
number them, though
I haven't the heart to

leave them (un)numbered
or to most of all deny
that numbering at their core

Jejune, all of these words are of people, anyway

ACT VI

AIN'T I A MADNESS?

. . . elsewhere called archaeology or case closed

X X ^X X X ^X

(
deep
log, these bones
a common lift   a self
mired in t)heft

Then again, such brutality, verbs tragic as the margins

<hr>

dossier these preferred four-letter words:
in case[x] I[x] come back here[x], to this distance & need[x] them[x]

start here with the stately pronoun again
the needle-and-thread frantic phone call
on the backsides of the years, I could call

harvest of birdsong on that corner alone
a madness, or I could call it the meddled re-
turn of forty-five mins., the clinking season

of rain, would you accept this collect call
from god knows where, a life now (re)fuse(d)
in the gutter, circus flags, a pending re-public,

ended as the heart should end or arise
in the flash-flooded air, a birthplace answ'ring
to unrecognizable versions of elsewhere

when I was young, Jejune gave I the rejected things
example: the breathable air; example: the clean sea
example: the plate w/ just 'nuff; example: the cryolite

any room, anyway, example: the mononuclear I
was a sea of graces, not peace or surface, I—raged,
I gathering sound for the mirror, Jejune, eventually

the trees will rush the river, inevitably the houses
will blot the map through one cynical night,
and what else, doudou darling, tell me anyway,

how you walk all these rivers, and is I feeling
the shudders of all the caves behind you
without forcing the point, will you tell the hounds

that they, too, are deeply wounded, are, too,
a sung-of citizen wrung out to dry in the felt-up
fields, disunity the blueprint of tanked-up roads

or call it a decorative cry, call it the wind jostling
the shutters with news of the circus animals, I among
them, the pigs, the hen, the cats trading our father

his language (languish) for the strange freedom of the dog
that in its short speech it keeps its doggedness a
small complaint, slogans in Heimlich manoeuvre

Jejune, all of these words are held to idols newly doomed, anyway

but let us not lock up this volt just yet
say the written thing is direct
a line to a nerve, one electric thing to another

perhaps this is why I can say the word love
to you, Jejune, and you will point at the mouth
and admit, there is its primitive ground, but the *pointing*

the tragedy of ampere things is all around us
and we must pretend this is new every time they
camera the vista with Laws making new goads

about our lives, we are not the sharpened things
they make of us, Jejune; here, drop your one
saved day into this one and let us meet us upright

have we eaten so many salt-preserved repasts
even now, even in the middle of this day, there's
no use dumping I into this bay, *I,* who'll bump that

track when they come for you, too; will your face
write willingly into the air when they are not
looking that you know i've been waiting here

at this corner to see you all day; do they search you
for whatever before they make the searching illegal,
what about that recipe for mum's coal-roasted kidney,

contraband of hallelujahs, the Shea soap she doctored
in the kitchen good enough an anti-inflammatory aid,
your mother's maiden name, some abortions, what

will they say about the usefulness of their endless
killing notations, what now, in this thin hour
have i faded from the miswritten main,

so when you call me Jejune, when you call me I
i'll say *Aye!* I will answer because to know we are
one in the same, to know this, this much

enough for the nights
in which to sleep well
this year, the next

the starving crowd has its talents, wordless corridors
famished for love or love's vocabularies, a cosmos
never tested in mud, a city in its rust-cultured tap

water, arcades of scrap, the most honest Ed's ever
been, rust, PVC, another whip, another route
to poor dreams, badges, name it: and just as soon

it disappears, a future paid in kàbán, watches
void of their work of keeping time, a minute
schism in a bottle's broken neck, a commerce

of annulled records, trees remembering fruit
the foolish work of asserting a thing, what
a hard thing, the freedom that bends the back

in an infinite series where we approach each oth'r
Jejune, forked in some road that might have
cropped up anyhow to cross us barely ready

or were we unaware that we had cracked I
to save us, split us three ways
as the centuries that made us possible left us

with all possible comprises, we have this one
existence, this so many elsewheres, in others,
I, and in every elsewhere, us both

and so you have arrived, Jejune, and so I
in a million pictures of our face, and still
I was not myself, i am not myself, myself

resembles something having nothing to do
with me and the idea that I would like
a holiday, a whole lifetime from this bend

where i have found my good sense
by its reach into my acceptance
or omuamua o moo ah moo ah

tout long kod ni bout how this must end
how dare the undead nerve in my ear
that does not behave as its length, it exists

to think about the echo one loses as a spaceship
elides spaceshit, we're responsible for the decom-
posting as the things I calls strange, things called mad

we give to no-one the shape of the shape
of the shape of a thing that light curves over time
length to width to depth and all of us its information

in the river's swelling urges, nothing drowns
but I sweep the perimeter, drowning
in my study of dreams, spent in their ordinary

unordinariness, their semblance of the world
their bargain to arrive judged by ended things
old money, new money, public executions, family

before brothers, before sisters built as beach forts
before I found blue vines in the trees crisscrossed
to swoops, swoops I would lie in and wait for onset

settled in familiar branches, branches with cold fruit
fruit for the shut mouth, how else to honour mothers
who claim no hunger in order to feed their children

children I would suffer if my names were big enough,
if I practised hanging upside down, taxonomically
through the world of waking newly through binoculars

how much is that life still worth, all the nickel-
and-diming, when the sweeping vultures are still
full vultures, even upside down, even binocular'd

I counted them; built fires from dry moss and seagrass
seagrass and dug bait, I dangled, dangled worms from
my hooked hand, hooked a great coral crab, left it

in my wooden trap, larger than my head, head I turn
over to check the sea's pulse, soon I'd have to give this
all back to the sea, throw even the sea back, sea that's

kept me loosed, followed as we've been, we in our sum-
mer of spent things, of met mothers, mothers who were
brothers, brothers who followed us here: who are here

as cloud, clouds as unsafe bridges, how to suffer rain,
the first drop and last drought, how the swollen hours
defy despair, sibilance of dreams, names to hum gently

reassembled limb by necessary limb, after mistaking
hallucinogenic mushrooms for regular mushrooms
I believe myself read, content for cheerful songs

I am not the first to begin here, in the hard silence
of forests, not the first to hear the gnashing
of roots into dirt, I've been less full of melody

I hear the birds abandon their branches, I mean
to suspend again, hollow and stately as suits
I mean the body a catalogue of bridges, Jejune,

whole towns, the body an abandonment of riches
the body afloat in flight at night, sure of nothing
but the pebbled paltriness of daydreams

here, a parade of haggard selves, in whose hands
the machete has found itself the flesh, I walk along
something still latent, dark, its embers prone to blaze suns

an ululating mouth here, a whimpering salvation
there, passé saboteurs dragged through the dark, is this
where life can carry over, is this the breeze through which

whole worlds reorder, postpone themselves, in the full-speed
collision of logic and opinion, the hard contradiction of missing
persons, of sterilized smiles in waiting rooms, in every endangered

language and other ways to invent the water, and other ways
to invent the water, and other ways to invent the water,
and other ways to invent the water, and other ways to invent

as if it were birch bark weary of the flame, kindness
ignited from the root, the foam-dry moss, mottle of
a cave's beachfront, release is always fiction-white

but let me not pass in its temper, as the red ants form
grommiers on someone's beaten lodge, in an hour
it will be reduced to planks, dark cedar paying off a debt

go past the boundary of the history you must soften
if it swells in you, rounds your belly, i am sorry, Jejune,
to have broken the seal of your embrace, to have stood

here and only watched you work in the darkness
in the complaint of the upkeep of their cottage
or a beach house, or hunger by any new name

here, the footstool's ten thousand folios between the locus
root, its strained rings thriving as the animus
of my practised mind, well, now stop this misery, this conceit

what use is the sky that floods our clemency of bones
it gives death that itinerant shove of the head
into the dark, hated instantly where it lands

bewildering the blôko, that love-shattered mirror
measuring the seasons, this world to fix by hand
my illegible hand overcrowds what I need to say

I cannot buy my writing hand, own hand, own act,
own thought, or I would perfect it, either is or ain't
a clearness of mind like that smogged city left behind

the maddening drum my father owns plays in steering time
its rhythms escape the eager day, like woven vats wandering
the market, or last wickets knocked down mid cricket match

i'm thinking of the great disease of this bill that coin and
the ladder he used at the base of the savannah stage in 1942
still there today, profane and revered, where he couldn't resist

what it resists now, the evolving rif' of the calypsonian's
threnody, and every eye, even the lens, even the pano-
rama of the country burned into I, leavening our meanings

the calming arrogance of dwindling enough to stay awake
through keeping wake, the entropic boons of the garden
called to live again: flatbush roses, tartan lilies, a shelter

the shape of a valley, its quiet breath after a storm
unexpected porcelain of scorpions, silk petals stacked
to Portuguese lace, the anagrammatic filter of coconut husks

aroma of rose water, marjoram balm, water cress, invitation
between lives, elliptical thirsts, what to recognize in these
half-needs, perplexing, these forgotten evenings of ablutions

okay, but this would kill, this neighbourhood
full of dogs at the post office, nothing so ordinary
as train tracks to let me move through the world

un-X-rayed, unfiltered, unvoiced in a vote
to know that woman singing at the entrance of the train
station, that muscular song she weaves, beg she outlives

the registers of her addictive refrain, if there's fog here
and someone's rags, here's evening too, and a mumbling,
few men, evening, here, evening in that voice but no train

if the day is always already begun, at what point does it break
what percentage of it survives our beheadings, or the bullets
travelling through the city lipping roll-ups, for 35.99 per hour

finding Black targets, helping along what must be condemned
water-stained ceilings, Black holes, unknowable scriptures, I
paralingual since the jump, folie à deux, that power-hungry

security guard pouring poison into his lover's half-drunk
bottle of misdiagnosis, at what point does the day's own
hand work itself enough to sleep or death or to whatever

how much and for how long, which human is psychic enough
which end to debate, whose rights to shed to innocence, given
Myself, given the long song i play, given the long day

the weekly diatribes of rainbows in the summer
how else to live, how else these leaps in logic
against a god obsessed with white, a god obsessed

this generic panic makes me want to throw paint
or paint the town aflame, if I had not stumbled
in this place, if homelessness, too simple a con-

di(c)tion for what I lived, if for the people who live
this still, who I now only glimpse through this wind-
shield, Myself, wanting to pull over, give them coffee

shave their chests, twist their hair into buns,
or more elegant things, needless that I should only
have new money, or old, or whatever to survive the iota

I tell you again, I am not my self, I resemble
amusement parks built for consolation
for our dusty interactions, for the mimic

Jejeune, all of these words microphone the wordless material anyway

for all of this, Jejune, does it matter from which
point the loose bond of our one heart strikes
the water with the force or fact of this now

not here or anywhere the inordinate ships dock
where a calibration of rags shapes our falling
where wealth of leaving, of return, is the voice
of nothings taking turns, whose signal

that we are being, mourned, or mercied into paper
trails approaching the dew as the water between
the first and last drought, notations of a desert

in the broken I or a comforted passerby, inviting:
Jejune, stay here and we will work as they who play,
stay on the toilet, think of all the lifetimes (how many?)

rolling into this one try, where we still walk the mile,
miles, steady how they're auctioned into the desert,
alive in the proof of ourselves, a nakedness, full-null

ACT VII

AIN'T I AGAIN?

. . . elsewhere called the hereafter, or it's just what we do

EPILOGUE

graph·eme
/'grafēm/
noun
LINGUISTICS

grapheme *is my usual predisposition the smallest meaningful contrastive unit
in a writing system such as I such as the study of proper names by the force of
all the wars that have preceded the pronoun taxonomically by dividing referents
into classes and classes such as the denomination of places, organizations, objects
into the slow world somewhere far from anywhere named Andromeda or a
new ideogram for someplace near here and really what is the word for belonging
to a common name first of her uvular vowel infinite of her kind & the care
that brings the well-known to distinguish one from all other identical beings let
alone the world in a familiar road or another road by anthem or automaton
or street by street animal by animal before the reonymy of rivers offsets their
given shape through their actual hydronymy or the alveolar* [PHONETICS] *lilt
of their assertion*

X^{XX}X^{XX}X

. . . utterly, utterly new

I am held within these claims: that I have kissed unlucky
things, buried pets, eaten sugar-free ice cream, endured a first
blood test, made friends without benefits, and lost them

found new ways of saying what is not ever enough to say
ways to fish, to drink, to park, to burn, to burn into
something new, with this life I have been careful

too much, disciplined to the extent of (dis)remembrance
infrequent colours pissed into the wind, I don't remember
when I decided to fold into my self, or when walking

foot before foot to the feeding ground of murderous birds
became the way to admit that words can be a giving up
outcome of years rearranging a subterranean scar

and I have been called many things late at night
greener grass, scientific utopia, dream of ancestors,
what about rainy weekends, what about poltroons,

the doomed cults full of hyper-rational people
who've miscalculated the height of doors, how many
stairs are left, and when stood up from a tumble

find polite applause, find the romance of liberal
consumption on the news, anyway, any sharp
thing is a short distance from possible to voluble

father, what about a foot laid down hard on the gloss
of the business-suited, the testing birds that remind
me I am just as committed to expression as to freedom

wet organ, the depth of the idea, the benign word
for denial would wipe out history, carefully let us
talk again, and if you will not hear me, consider

the coral crab, my wooden trap, the sung-of citizen
hung out to dry, consider I, consider me, I keep
one vat of tar alive for any possible crack needing

fixed by hand, I have come before, wholly atypical
with the volume turned up, way up on the radio,
let me pause here, I am not here if not diagonal

let me start where it begins, with Jejune, with I,
who went to see my father, blinded in his inborn
peri-cranial debris, redblack, purpleblack, newblack

ultrablack, black-black light, *definitely not partially*
blind, he says, he with his gone sight scarring
the ceiling with the uneasy movements of his eyes

I had to look up, had to fall into this museum
of once-useful things, boxes of matches, stark
prevalence of spent days I can't remember now

except how bright: yellow, blue, green, red, the brown
and rust, and the still-mortared wooden beams, manman,
I called his name, *dada, sa'k ka fête?*, I watched him know

my voice, cut through the way-high volume of his stereo
as though to enter myself, how I enter the hot-house
of his bedroom, his whole life nearly cordoned now

I watch my father search for my name
I watch my father knowing my voice
I watch my father remembering my face

I watch the confirming movement of his hands
considering me, there, wholly uncharacteristic
consider me as a certain elasticity you can enter

the ordinariness of the waves, the scar debating
an end to its pathology, the basic fabric living
recaptured ideals, scared, justement, as a man

needing to remember his seed by voice, to make
and leave fortunes, (un)exchangeable outside
of Myself, I am always leaving

I am not always distinct upon return, this is the eye
that sees where I cannot enter, the eye which is
wholly blind, I lie down on his fibrous carpet

and simply fall back into Myself, once Jejune,
as the bones in my chest heave their lodging
through skin, here the eye's impossibilities

make corridors of things not too long arriving
the coulomb of an organ most aware of lethal
temperatures, to prompt us both into the words

that have been made into supper for us, turning out
a needed hour or more, turning out the yellow of even-
tides, into the vast haul of nature that keeps us feeling

there is in his yard three beautiful pomegranate trees
one bears diseased fruit, the other two are not to blame,
all full of birds, let me get back to the thing that must be said

wearing a T-shirt, beads, a feather, a poesy on my head,
impossible, Jejune, this talk of the living unconcerned with
our dead, in one type of Earth, I suppose, is a tangle of roots

and a tangle of roots is a prayer or something, I have no way
of knowing, except to agree that when the ballasts of who we
are must be measured not everything will do, not everything,

but sometimes to abolish what's trapped inside a diseased
pomegranate, a too-young pomegranate, is what reminds
the birds into the goaded lift before planting permanently

let us both suppose, too, that to come upon so many birds
all trapped in agreement, or some scant accord, is murder
to come upon in you, all of the living, all that is yet tacit

is first to be unafraid to caw, and I suppose, to be feathered
apart, in the reverberations of that account, you see, it is
the eye turning our years, to come this far is to admit this

and that every remnant thing is a kind of life, some of it
living, some of it yet dead, like mother's scent, mother's
bone, mother's stitched cesarean, mother's knee, post-rain,

to the burial ground, all in a basket woven of palm
the yielding dampness of dirt, buried throughout the world
beneath the pomegranate tree that bears the restless fruit

whatever it is, it is not too dehydrated to hold
what is mine, the twenty-first century is mine
and what does this say of les jeunes, untiring

telling me what to look for, what species do not
need me to survive, certainly not my split tongue
needing touch and language, in this blank catalogue

of reassembled lives, misassembled lives, unass-
embled days, I am a/part and some thoughts are
easy: pretend to be isolated, stress an accumulation

of disappearances, one way to transform and two
and three, all the griefs that I have grieved, how
they turn the head quickly away again,

birth, too, is accidental, whether in islands or the eye's
retaliating spasms, some dead man, his hurt and zeal
protoconforming; they will sue the world for a lack

of peace, to want to live in a world my own hand
has made, not hands too aware of their wild plots
just one hand in the world, meeting other hands

in crowds full of morning-pleasant heads
whipping out greetings, and soon an angular woman
who'll offer me that chance, her limp-loosed hand

and I should shake it as a bundle meant to be carried
in both hands, several decades past due, past indecisive
jurors, past nostalgic feudalism, internet profiles of the already dead

let me tell you who and what else
escapes danger by ordinariness,
that when someone calls with news

of safety, I acquiesce to the old rhythms
of lightness, waking up thrown from
the orbit of once-forgivable things

a city is time for me, so I cut the road
I exit that spastic age, pamphletless
that decade, I reject

what would train the eye away from the normalizing
whim of credentials, confusing the word philanderer
with philanthropist, confusing the word incest with incest

to say unsee and then remake, to say remake and then unsee
to say we is to oblige the sun its rays, to say we have
witnessed enough, to say we partook, to say we have endured

to say we know the bitter knowledge of fucking up
to say all of our giants are dying, the birds now
congregate in weeping, following our languaged times

to say to you well done, to say to you I cannot stop
the blows, how they hush and swell outside of any
guilt, it has been a time and now I must leap

to be blown open, mixed-in I, blown-open I,
loud-noise I, lightning in the brain I, music-making
I imagine surprise one morning, alone,

imagine a door, no house to address, imagine
the sudden door, a broken thing illuminated,
and you would rather leave than spend the night,

imagine the blank manoeuvres of coming home,
sleeping on the top stair of that Parkdale
building in mid-February, that or you spend the night

on King Street, stretched against your protected limits,
on the lawn of a sea-spanning country, a sung-of
citizen, flung out to freeze, from what formlessness

I was that speck in the halogen confusion of myself
If I were once planted in dirt, if I were once the taste
of wood after mourning, the split-tongue of the long

beast out of water, another bête belonging to something
bigger than a point of view, wider than this expanse
of doors mapping the incalculable coasts of Black continents,

I was that speck in the multiplier of myself
déjà vu, an early stage, what I have learned, new langu-
age held in the nowhere of my blood up against the page

and the dread thing is that I forget and must do it
all again, a dyzgraph^{x}st, je connais, justement—
I, (re)done when the world itself awakes again

as I take a last picture of you as before, this time
        Jejune, now one hundred years and fluent in Hausa—
the shutter will keep something of you inside it,

it is better this way, or I would have no reason at all to write you
what folds your ear sideways to my mouth, I to slip into,
wondering what we might have become were we not so alive

NOTES

Companions—in-person, virtual, textual, and otherwise anchored this writing. Poets, musicians, painters, writers, and thinkers. Many years of thinking and reading and learning have turned out things both calculable and otherwise, here. Thank you in all ways, to those named and unnamed, because the mind does not always grasp its own maps as conscious.

My foremost companions:

Simone Swartz-Bart, (through *The Bridge of Beyond*, aiding pages 133–134);
Dionne Brand (through *The Blue Clerk*, aiding pages 107, 108, 120);
Fred Moten (originator of the Blur, and the disembodied eyes throughout);
Saidiya Hartman; Kamau Brathwaite (for wayward departures);
Kevin Adonis Browne (for the deep listening traveling on page 131, 137);
Patrick Chamoiseau (through *Texaco*, aiding pages 136, 137);
Juliane Okot Bitek (Gauntlet inspired the footnoting in ACT V);
Anna L-P (for the line carrying electricity on page 124);
Rinaldo Walcott and Édouard Glissant (thinking kinship through *Queer Returns* and *Poetics of Relation* respectively);
Nicole Sealey ("I was not myself, i am not myself, myself/ resembles something having nothing to do/ with me" is adapted from "cento for the night I said, "i love you" from her collection, *Ordinary Beast*);
Tracey Lindberg (for the portmanteau bigbeautiful);
Liz Howard, Eliza Robertson (how you talk the cosmos);

The musics of: Nicholas Payton, James Brandon Lewis, Robert Glasper, Mammal Hands;
So many hours of expansive self-splitting paint-think with the work of Basquiat;

*The Dyzgraph*ˣ*st* as concept, figure and being owes a great debt to Christina Sharpe, through her book *In the Wake: On Blackness and Being*. Further thinking, again, with *Monstrous Intimacies: Making Post-Slavery Subjects*.

Some parts of this work were previously published in Lemonhound and Poemeleon (Canada) though they appear here in this work reconstituted or entirely reconfigured.

ACKNOWLEDGEMENTS

KM, KM, MM—always, love.

Maggie. Phoebe. Paul.

Dionne Brand: your editing found the book, kept the pen inked, tuned every line, every syllable. In every language: Every thanks.

Kelly Joseph, this poem knows better than I do how much you work for poetry and poets in your capacity as publishing manager of M&S. You saw *The Dyzgraph*^x*st* through more than I know. There is an ode here, which is yours.

Jared Bland, thanks for all of your great work as publisher of M&S.

Leah Springate, you've created a brilliant book design and an outstanding book cover. Thank you.

Sean Tai, typesetter; Valentina Capuani and Kimberlee Hesas; Ruta Liormonas, publicist, and Peter Norman, copy editor: so much gratitude.

Sandra Brewster's Blur 9 (3/3) is on the cover of this book. Thank you, Sandra. What a conversation this is turning out for us.

Deep appreciation to Juliane Okot Bitek, Vladimir Lucien, Nick Makoha, Nicole Sealey, and Safiya Sinclair.

Thank you, dear readers. I and i and I and you.

The ocean drama roves by the movement of a multitude in it. Thank you.